Eyes on the Sky

D1520140

Neptune

by Don Nardo

KIDHAVEN PRESS

THOMSON

GALE

Detroit • New York • San Diego • San Francisco
Boston • New Haven, Conn. • Waterville, Maine
London • Munich

Library of Congress Cataloging-in-Publication Data

Nardo, Don, 1947–
  Neptune / by Don Nardo.
    p. cm.—(Eyes on the sky)
  Includes bibliographical references.
  Summary: Discusses the discovery of Neptune as well
  as its topography and the search for water and life.
    ISBN 0-7377-1001-2 (hardback : alk. paper)
    1. Neptune (Planet)—Juvenile literature. [1. Neptune
  (Planet)] I. Title. II. Series.
    QB691 .N37   2002
    523.48'1—dc21

2001004588

Cover and Title Page Photo: Hulton/Archive by Getty Images
© AFP/CORBIS, 20
© Yann Arthus-Bertrand/CORBIS, 42
© Bettmann/CORBIS, 25
© CORBIS, 28 (left), 29
Corel Corporation, 32, 38, 39
FPG International, 14
© D. Robert & Lorri Franz/CORBIS, 34 (left)
Getty Images, 17
© Jeremy Horner/CORBIS, 12
Hulton/Archive by Getty Images, 9, 16
Jet Propulsion Laboratory, 21 (right), 28 (right)
Chris Jouan, 23
Chris Jouan and Martha Schierholz, 5
Mary Evans Picture Library, 6
© NASA/Roger Ressmeyer/CORBIS, 21 (left), 31
Brandy Noon, 8, 10-11, 18, 27, 37, 40
© Roger Ressmeyer/CORBIS, 34 (right), 35

Copyright 2002 by KidHaven Press,
an imprint of The Gale Group
10911 Technology Place, San Diego, CA 92127

No part of this book may be reproduced or used in any other
form or by any other means, electrical, mechanical, or other-
wise, including, but not limited to, photocopying, recording, or
any information storage and retrieval system, without prior
written permission from the publisher.

Table of Contents

1
Neptune's Discovery

In 1781 English astronomer William Herschel discovered the **planet** Uranus, which brought the number of known planets in the **solar system** to seven. (The solar system is made up of the sun and all of the objects that move around it.) Mercury is the closest planet to the sun; then Venus, Earth, Mars, Jupiter, and Saturn.

The newly discovered planet, Uranus, which lies beyond Saturn, is the only one that requires a telescope to see. It stood to reason that if any planets lay beyond Uranus, they would be even fainter and harder to find. Indeed, finding the eighth planet—Neptune—took another sixty-five years. The quest involved a large number of researchers. It also resembled a very long detective story because these men were trying to solve a strange cosmic mystery; and some of them made mistakes or suffered tragic misfortunes, causing the search to drag on and on. The final result, however, was the discovery of Neptune by a combination of clever means and dogged hard work. This achievement still ranks as one of the great triumphs of modern science.

Uranus's Misbehavior

At the time that Herschel found Uranus, no one had any idea if other planets existed beyond it. But over time, some astronomers began to suspect that at least one more planet was lurking in the dark depths of space. The reason they believed this was that Uranus behaved rather strangely. In the years following its discovery, researchers observed its motion and calculated its **orbit** (its path around the sun). But as the years went by, the planet did

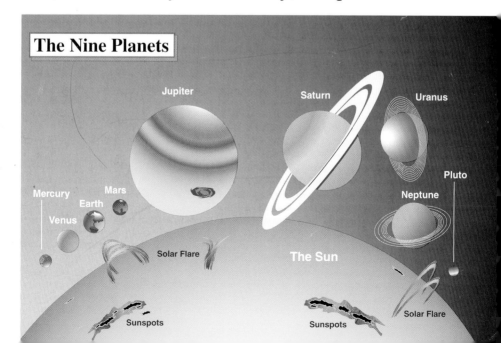

The Nine Planets

Jupiter

Saturn

Uranus

Pluto

Mercury

Mars

Earth

Neptune

Venus

Solar Flare

The Sun

Sunspots

Sunspots

Solar Flare

English astronomer William Herschel discovered the planet Uranus.

not follow the predicted orbit. It strayed farther and farther from the path plotted for it, and no one could figure out why.

One possibility for Uranus's odd behavior was that the original calculations had been in error. So in 1820 French mathematician Alexis Bouvard carefully calculated a new orbit for Uranus. However, the planet did not follow this new path either. By 1832 Uranus was noticeably off course again. This time no one could claim the math was wrong. In that year, one of the world's leading astronomers, George Airy, director of England's Cambridge Observatory, offered a solution to the mystery. Perhaps, he said, the laws of **gravity** did not work the same in the outer reaches of the solar system. If so, that might explain why the math that worked for the closer planets would not work for Uranus.

Some astronomers were not satisfied with this explanation. They saw no reason to suppose that the laws of nature worked differently from one part of the universe to another. In 1834 another English scientist, T.J. Hussey, discussed the problem with Bouvard. And they agreed on a different explanation for Uranus's misbehavior. In November of that year Hussey wrote to Airy and proposed that an unknown planet must lie beyond Uranus. The gravity of this planet, said Hussey, was pulling on Uranus. This was the mysterious force that was keeping Uranus from following its predicted orbit.

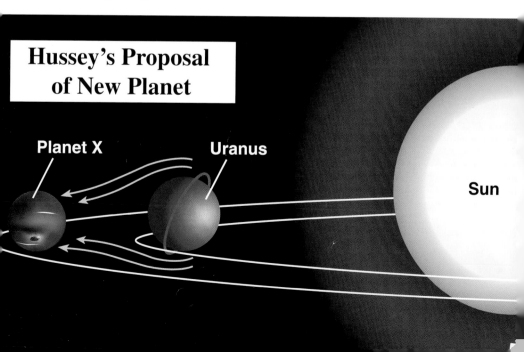

Hussey's Proposal of New Planet

Planet X   Uranus

Sun

An Enormously Difficult Problem

In theory, it was possible to find the position of the unknown planet by observing Uranus's movements. But the math involved was enormously difficult and time consuming. No computers or other mechanical calculators yet existed; and every one of the thousands of complex math problems had to be done by hand, then checked and rechecked.

For reasons that are uncertain, Hussey and Bouvard did not undertake this daunting task. They hoped that Airy, a fine mathematician, would do it. But he mistakenly assumed he would first have to observe at least two complete revolutions of Uranus around the sun. The problem was that Uranus takes 84 years to orbit the sun once. So in Airy's view, it would be almost 170 years before enough data was available to find the unknown planet. For this reason, he did not even try to find it.

Meanwhile, some other researchers independently came to the same conclusion Hussey and Bouvard had. In 1840, brilliant German astronomer Friedrich Bessel decided that a new planet lay beyond Uranus. He assigned the laborious job of computing its position to one of his pupils, Friedrich Flemming. But Flemming soon died unexpectedly. And when Bessel tried to pick up where Flemming left off, he became seriously ill and had to stop.

The following year, a twenty-two-year-old English college student— John Couch Adams— attacked the same problem on his own. He tried to eliminate a great deal of time and effort by plugging **Bode's Law** into his calculations. Bode's Law was named after Johann Bode, the

Englishman John Couch Adams worked out Neptune's approximate position in 1845.

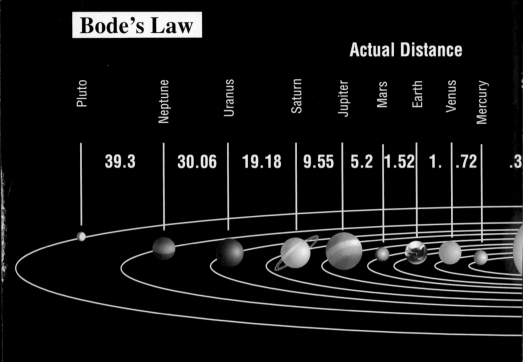

Bode's Law

Actual Distance

Pluto	Neptune	Uranus	Saturn	Jupiter	Mars	Earth	Venus	Mercury
39.3	30.06	19.18	9.55	5.2	1.52	1.	.72	.3

German astronomer who, in the 1700s, pointed out that the spacing of the known planets followed a rough but unusually regular pattern. Starting with Mercury, the closest to the sun, each successive planet was about twice as far from the sun as the one before it. So Adams began with the assumption that the unknown planet orbited about twice as far from the sun as Uranus did.

Adams Locates the Planet

By working diligently, by September 1845 Adams had worked out a tentative position for the new planet. All he needed was an astronomer with a large telescope to look at that area of the sky and confirm the object's existence. This turned out

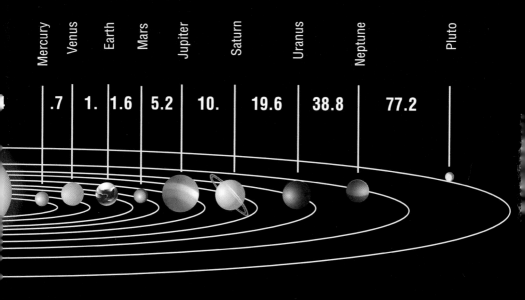

Bode's Prediction

Mercury	Venus	Earth	Mars	Jupiter	Saturn	Uranus	Neptune		Pluto
.7	1.	1.6	5.2	10.	19.6	38.8	77.2		

to be easier said than done, however. Adams approached Airy's successor at Cambridge Observatory, James Challis. But Challis claimed he was too busy.

So Adams tried Airy, the chief astronomer at the world famous Greenwich Observatory. Unfortunately, both times that Adams made the trip to Greenwich, Airy was unable to meet with him. Adams left his calculations for the Astronomer Royal to examine. But Airy did not think that a man so young and inexperienced as Adams could solve so difficult a problem. So once again Airy failed to act. If only he had taken the time to look through his telescope, he would have gone down in history as the discoverer of the eighth planet. The position Adams

Greenwich Observatory, in Greenwich, England, where that nation's Astronomer Royal works.

had calculated was fewer than two degrees off the mark, a very small amount of error!

Because of Airy's inaction, the honor of making the great discovery fell to other scientists. In the same year Adams computed the planet's position, French mathematician Urbain J.J. Leverrier began working on the same problem. Leverrier, who knew nothing about Adams's work, quickly found the solution. In September 1846 Leverrier wrote to highly respected German astronomer Johann Gottfried Galle. Leverrier implored Galle to undertake a telescopic search for the planet in a specific area of the sky.

A New Member of the Sun's Family

In the evening of September 23, 1846, Galle and his assistant, Heinrich Louis d'Arrest, began the search. It took a mere hour. Suddenly, in the midst of hundreds of stars—which appeared as tiny pinpoints of light—Galle saw a small, fuzzy, bluish-colored disk. Breathless with excitement, he notified Leverrier. The planet the Frenchman had located using mathematics alone actually existed!

Because he had found the planet's position, Leverrier had the honor of naming it. He chose Neptune, the ancient Roman name for

Neptune's bluish-colored disk floats in a tiny patch of the star-studded night sky.

the god of the seas. Perhaps he was partly motivated by the object's ocean-blue color.

Soon, astronomers across the globe trained their telescopes on the newest member of the sun's family. Thanks to the great William Herschel, by now an old man, Adams's efforts to find the planet became public. Airy's and Challis's failure to act on Adams's calculations also came out. English scientists and newspaper editors attacked Airy and Challis, saying it was their fault that England had lost the race to find Neptune.

Luckily, there were no such hard feelings between Adams and Leverrier. They met at Herschel's estate in 1847 and became friends. Though history gives the credit for Neptune's discovery to Leverrier and Galle, Adams has not been forgotten. The remarkable story of how two great minds, working independently, solved the same mystery at the same time will be told and retold for ages to come.

2
Shaped by Dynamic Forces

After Neptune's discovery in 1846, astronomers determined its orbit, size, distance from the sun, and diameter. They also discovered two moons orbiting the planet. But for a long time, it was not possible to learn much more about Neptune. Its average distance from the sun is almost 2.8 billion miles. That is a little more than thirty times the distance at which Earth orbits the sun. Neptune is so remote that even in the largest telescopes it long appeared as no more than a tiny bluish disk. So the planet and its satellites remained wrapped in a veil of mystery.

All this changed in 1989. That year the Voyager 2 spacecraft, launched in 1977 by the National Aeronautics and Space Administration

An artist's conception of the Voyager 2 spacecraft approaching Neptune in 1989.

(NASA), flew by Neptune. The spacecraft's cameras snapped dozens of detailed photos of the planet. For the first time, people glimpsed Neptune up close. And a world of incomparable beauty was revealed. Voyager also discovered several more moons orbiting the planet. In the 1990s the Hubble Space Telescope (HST) began operation. Orbiting high above Earth's surface, the HST has taken hundreds of close-up photos of Neptune. Thanks to Voyager and the HST, today the veil of mystery that once shrouded the eighth planet has partially lifted.

The Outermost Gas Giant

Voyager and the HST confirmed some important facts about Neptune that scientists had earlier deduced. First, the planet is very large. Its diameter is 30,760 miles (49,500 km), about 3.9 times wider than Earth. If Neptune were hollow, it could hold about sixty objects the size of Earth.

Also, Neptune is composed mostly of gases and liquids. For this reason, astronomers often refer to it as a "**gas giant**." It is the smallest and outermost of four gas giants orbiting in the outer reaches of the solar system. (The first three, beginning with the largest and closest to the sun, are Jupiter, Saturn, and Uranus.)

The planets of the solar system, including the four gas giants. Moving right from Jupiter (center), are Saturn, Uranus, and Neptune.

Forming the Gas Giants

These huge planets formed from millions of small objects called **planetesimals**, which orbited the sun when the solar system was young. Gravity made the planetesimals combine into larger clumps. The largest clumps of all became the planets. Gases and ices were more abundant in the outer solar system than in the inner solar system. So the gravities of Jupiter, Saturn, Uranus, and Neptune pulled in vast amounts of gas and ice. As these planets heated up, the ices melted into liquids and more gases.

The Windiest Planet

As a result of this process, the four gas giants have no solid surfaces, as Earth and other inner planets do. (That means that a spacecraft from Earth visiting Neptune would have no place to land.) Instead, Neptune's inner core is made up of a very **dense** (highly compact) mixture of gases and liquids. These include melted rock, water, and two poisonous gases—**ammonia** and **methane**.

Because Neptune's outer region is less dense, scientists refer to it as the planet's atmosphere. It is made up mainly of water, methane, and nature's two lightest gases—hydrogen and helium. The methane gives the planet its bluish

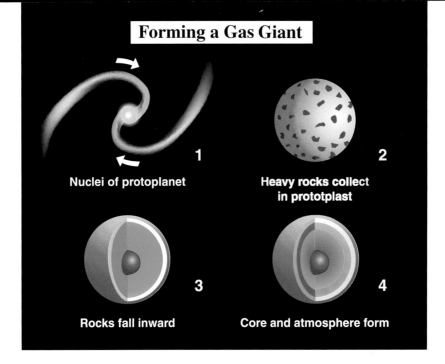

Forming a Gas Giant

1 — Nuclei of protoplanet

2 — Heavy rocks collect in prototplast

3 — Rocks fall inward

4 — Core and atmosphere form

tone. (The individual particles—or molecules—of methane absorb the reddish rays of the sun; the bluish rays are reflected.) At the top of the atmosphere, near the edge of space, it is very cold. So some of the methane freezes into tiny crystals. These methane ice crystals form white clouds, some of them quite large. Voyager scientists nicknamed one large, very bright cloud "Scooter" because it moved rapidly through the atmosphere.

The Windiest Planet

Scooter was not the only moving feature Voyager saw on Neptune. In fact, the planet is extremely **dynamic** (active). The gases, liquids, and ice clouds in its atmosphere are constantly moving. So are some huge hurricane-like storms. When

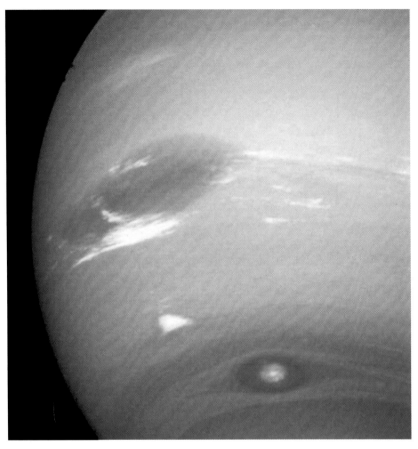

The long white cloud called "Scooter" passes near Neuptune's Great Dark Spot.

Voyager flew by the planet in 1989, it photographed such a storm. It came to be known as the Great Dark Spot: a massive, dark-gray, oval shaped feature as large as Earth, **rotating** (spinning) from right to left. Astronomers compared the Great Dark Spot to Jupiter's Great Red Spot, a storm three times the width of Earth. Voyager also revealed a smaller storm in Neptune's upper atmosphere, which they dubbed DS2.

The Great Dark Spot, DS2, methane clouds, and other features in Neptune's atmosphere whip along at tremendous speeds. Some move westward at up to 745 miles (1,200 km) per hour; others move almost twice that fast, more than twice the speed of sound. That makes Neptune the windiest planet in the solar system.

The causes of these fantastic winds are not yet completely understood. One theory suggests that they occur because of the way the planet rotates on its axis. Neptune's heaviest section—its core—rotates in little more than sixteen hours. That means that a day on the eighth planet is sixteen hours long (compared with a twenty-four-hour day on earth). However,

Jupiter's Great Red Spot (left) is a large storm like Neptune's Great Dark Spot, (right).

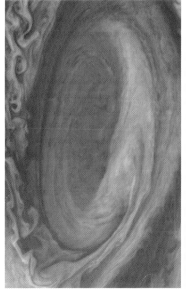 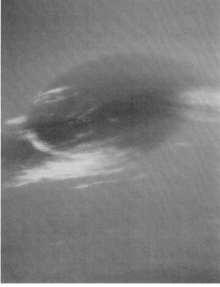

Neptune's lighter atmosphere rotates somewhat slower than its core. As plumes of gas rise from below, they suddenly slow and fall behind the fast-moving core. The core rotates eastward; while in relation to the core, the atmosphere falls back toward the west. A great deal of energy is created in this process, and that energy drives the winds.

A Huge Methane Engine

The forces creating Neptune's supersonic winds are not the only dynamic processes at work on the planet. An enormous methane cycle constantly breaks apart and re-forms molecules of methane. The process begins when the sun's rays break down methane molecules floating in Neptune's upper atmosphere. These pieces are molecules of gasoline-like substances. These soon freeze into tiny ice crystals. Then the crystals gently drift and fall deeper into the atmosphere, where it is warmer. Here, the ice melts back into gases, which sink still deeper.

When the gasoline-like gases reach denser regions, where the pressure is great, they mix with hydrogen and turn back into methane. Some of this methane rises up into the upper atmosphere. And the cycle then repeats itself. In this way, none of Neptune's methane is lost. In a way, the eighth planet is like a huge

The Methane Cycle

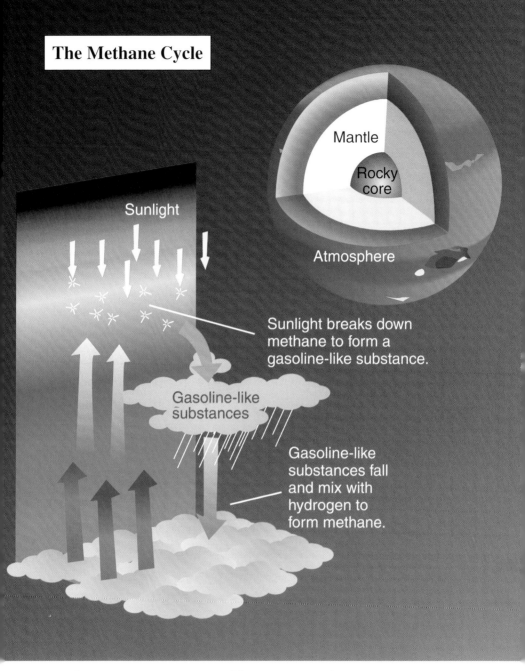

Mantle

Rocky core

Atmosphere

Sunlight

Sunlight breaks down methane to form a gasoline-like substance.

Gasoline-like substances

Gasoline-like substances fall and mix with hydrogen to form methane.

methane engine. A self-contained system continually rebuilding itself, it has orbited in the solar system's dark depths for billions of years. It will continue to do so for many billions more.

3
Neptune's Planetary System

Voyager 2 provided many surprises during its historic flyby of Neptune in 1989. Perhaps the most exciting of these was that the planet does not orbit alone in the vast, dark gulf beyond Uranus. Just as the sun has a family of orbiting objects—the solar system—Neptune has a large and complex planetary system.

Scientists had long known about two of Neptune's moons. In October 1846, about a month after the planet's discovery, English astronomer William Lassell found Triton. And American astronomer G.P. Kuiper discovered Nereid in 1949. (In ancient Greek mythology, both Triton and Nereid were sea gods, like Neptune.) But for well more than a century, these moons appeared in telescopes as mere specks of light. It seemed that

Neptune did not have much of a family of its own. So no one was quite prepared for the spectacular number, complexity, and beauty of the objects Voyager detected around the planet.

The Minor Satellites

Among the new wonders Voyager revealed in the Neptunian system were six more moons. Along with Nereid, they brought the total of the planet's known minor satellites to seven. The second largest of the seven is Proteus, also named after an ancient Greek sea god. At 250 miles (400 km) in diameter, Proteus is actually larger than Nereid. Why, then, could Nereid, but not Proteus, be seen from Earth? The answer is that Proteus is much closer to Neptune

American astronomer G.P. Kuiper discovered Neptune's moon Nereid.

than Nereid. Proteus orbits its parent at a distance of only 57,700 miles (92,800 km), a little more than twice the distance around the Earth. So in earthly telescopes, the moon was lost in the bright glare of Neptune's much larger disk.

Nereid is not all that much smaller than Proteus. Nereid is about 210 miles (340 km) across. That is about one-tenth the diameter of Earth's moon. Nereid is also the farthest of Neptune's satellites from the planet's cloudtops. What makes Nereid particularly strange, though, is that its distance from Neptune varies considerably. It comes as close as 841,100 miles (1,353,600 km) from the planet; then it swings out on a long, narrow orbit to a distance of 5,980,200 miles (9,623,700 km).

This odd behavior suggests that Nereid is a captured body. It may originally have been one of the ancient planetesimals from which the planets were built. Perhaps it strayed close enough for Neptune's gravity to hold it fast, but not close enough to crash into the planet.

The other five minor moons orbiting Neptune are Larissa, with a diameter of 64 miles (104 km); Galatea (49 miles, or 79 km); Despina (46 miles, or 74 km); Thalassa (25 miles, or 40 km); and Naiad (18 miles, or 29 km). All seven minor satellites are irregularly shaped rather than **spherical** (round). This is because

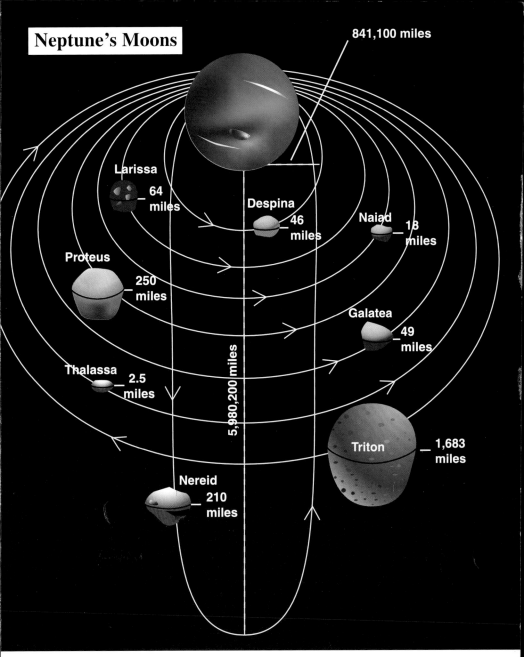

Neptune's Moons

841,100 miles

Larissa — 64 miles

Despina — 46 miles

Naiad — 18 miles

Proteus — 250 miles

Galatea — 49 miles

Thalassa — 2.5 miles

5,980,200 miles

Triton — 1,683 miles

Nereid — 210 miles

the **mass** (total amount of matter) of each is not enough for its gravity to crush its materials into a sphere. These seven moons all circle Neptune in the same direction the planet rotates—toward the east.

Triton—A Strange and Fascinating World

In striking contrast, Neptune's single major moon, Triton, is unlike the minor moons in nearly all respects. First, Triton is very large as planetary moons go. It is 1,680 miles (2,705 km) across, about three-quarters the diameter of Earth's moon. Also like Earth's moon, Triton is massive enough to be spherical in shape.

Another major difference between Triton and Neptune's minor moons is that Triton orbits the planet in the opposite direction—from east to west. Astronomers call this **retrograde** (backward) **motion.** If Triton had formed near and at the same time as

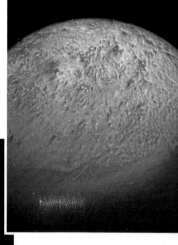

One of Neptune's smaller moons is barely visible above the planet (left); above is the largest, Triton.

Neptune, it would move in the same direction the planet rotates. So only one logical explanation exists for the satellite's strange retrograde motion. Like Nereid, Triton must be a captured body. Probably, Triton once orbited closer to the sun. Then the gravity of one of the other gas giants pushed it out toward Neptune, which snared it with its own gravity.

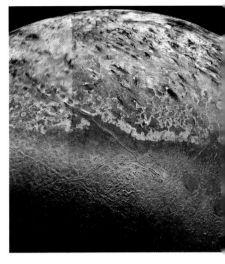

Strange dark spots and blotches cover the surface of Triton.

This scenario would explain some of the bizarre surface features Voyager photographed on Triton. Much of the moon's surface looks like the skin of a cantaloupe, with uneven light and dark spots and blotches. Several lakes of frozen water are also visible. Triton appears to be made up largely of water, nitrogen, and methane ices, with some rocks mixed in. Oddly, these ices are marred by very few **impact craters** like those visible on Earth's moon.

These facts suggest that Triton was and remains very active. Astronomers think that when Neptune captured Triton, the planet's huge gravity caused the moon's interior to melt. Gases and fluids bubbled up to the surface.

Bursting gas bubbles produced the spots and blotches; and liquid water gushed up and formed lakes, which then froze. This volcanic-like activity filled in most impact craters that existed on the surface.

Moreover, Triton's surface is still active and constantly changing. Voyager detected two large plumes of nitrogen gas shooting up from the moon's icy ground. The plumes were moving faster than 300 miles per hour. A small amount of the gas from such eruptions spreads out and forms a thin atmosphere. Scientists estimate that it is only about 1/70,000 as thick as Earth's atmosphere. Still, it can create clouds of nitrogen ice crystals, which float a few miles above the surface.

Neptune's Ring System

Besides the eight moons, Neptune's planetary system features a set of rings encircling the planet. This is not surprising considering that the other three gas giants have ring systems, too. (Saturn's is the largest and most famous, of course.) In the 1980s, shortly before Voyager's flyby, astronomers suspected that Neptune might have rings. The spacecraft confirmed this fact, showing four separate rings. The outermost and brightest ring lies about 39,000 miles (62,900 km) from Neptune's center. The

Two of Netpune's faint rings are visible in this photo taken by Voyager 2.

other three rings orbit closer, the innermost one touching the planet's cloudtops.

Neptune's rings are composed mostly of dust. They are very faint and difficult to see. Scientists think that they formed hundreds of millions of years ago when two of the planet's satellites collided. (Or perhaps a comet or other cosmic body smashed into one of the moons.) Over time, the fragments of the disaster collided over and over again, producing dust with a few small chunks of rock mixed in. The best estimate is that altogether the rings contain enough material to make up a moon about three miles wide. This is very small and explains why Neptune's rings are so thin and faint. If the much larger Proteus or Larissa were to break apart, the planet would acquire a ring system rivaling Saturn's.

Thanks to Voyager, Neptune has finally revealed its rings, moons, and some of its other secrets to human observers. Undoubtedly, the ocean-blue planet has still other surprises in store. But these will have to wait until other spacecraft make the long trip to the eighth planet's lonely realm.

A NASA space shuttle blasts off. Scientists hope that such a craft will one day visit Neptune.

4

Could Life Exist on Neptune?

Until the last couple of decades, most scientists seriously doubted that life could exist on worlds markedly different than Earth. The idea of life on Neptune and on the other gas giants certainly seemed unthinkable. First, these planets have no solid surfaces for living things to grow in or walk on. Second, they are made up to a large extent of poison gases. And third, because they lie far from the sun, they are very cold. For these reasons, the chances for life as we know it on Neptune seemed remote indeed.

But what about life as we do *not* know it? Some scientists have come to believe that life of some kind might be able to adapt to extreme physical conditions. This is actually the case on

On Earth, polar bears (top) thrive in cold places; life also exists in hot volcanic vents (bottom).

Earth. Living things fill every conceivable niche on the planet. Some plants and animals thrive in the freezing arctic seas and ice sheets; others exist under tremendous pressures at the bottoms of the oceans; and bacteria and other living creatures dwell inside steaming hot volcanic vents or where there is little or no air. It seems at least possible, then, that some kind of life might have taken hold in one or both of two places in the Neptunian system.

The Building Blocks of Life

The first of these two places is in the atmosphere of Neptune itself. Several years ago, the now-deceased famous astronomer Carl Sagan pointed out that life might exist in Jupiter's atmosphere. Jupiter's cloud layers contain hydrogen, oxygen, nitrogen, carbon, and water in varying amounts. These are the same basic substances that support life on Earth. Many of these materials were brought by comets that crashed into Jupiter over the course of billions of years. Many comets have collided with the other gas giants, too. So these same life-supporting substances are found in the atmosphere of Neptune.

Another, more exotic possibility exists. Perhaps life on a gas giant does not need all of the substances earthly life does. All life on Earth is based to one degree or another on the element carbon. Carbon molecules combine with other elements to produce the complex

The late astronomer Carl Sagan (left) proposed that life might exist in Jupiter's clouds.

molecules that make up the building blocks of life. However, some scientists have suggested that alien life might be based on some other element. Silicon (a major component of rocks and sand on Earth) easily combines with a number of other elements. Another possibility is ammonia, which exists in large quantities on the gas giants.

Creatures That Ride the Air Currents

The first consideration is where in Neptune's atmosphere such life could thrive. The deeper one goes into the planet, the more pressure one encounters. Too much pressure might destroy complex molecules before they can develop into living things. On the other hand, it might be too cold in the upper reaches of Neptune's atmosphere to support life. However, the zone in between these extremes features both warmth and moderate pressures.

The planet's howling winds must also be considered. These might be too violent an environment for life to develop. The winds are worst, though, near Neptune's equator. Near the planet's poles, the atmosphere is calmer. This would be the most likely place to find Neptunian life.

What would such atmospheric life be like? Dr. Sagan and other scientists proposed the theory that simple, rootless plants might float leisurely along on air currents. Over time, other versions of such plants might have developed roots. The waste materials and dead bodies of earlier generations might form small clods of material in which later generations take root. Colonies of these plants could drift along in air currents, fragmenting from time to time; each piece would form a new colony.

Aerial animals could also exist in Neptune's warmer, calmer atmospheric currents. Balloonlike or jellyfish-like creatures could ride the winds. They might also learn to maneuver on their own through the principle of jet propulsion. Such a creature might suck in air from a mouth or nose hole in the front and

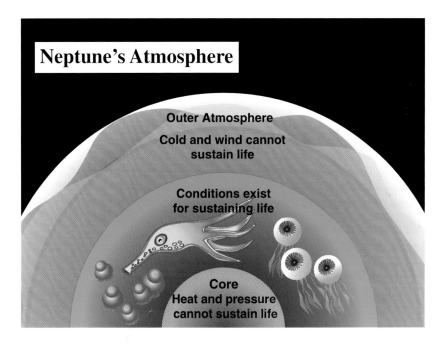

Neptune's Atmosphere

Outer Atmosphere
Cold and wind cannot sustain life

Conditions exist for sustaining life

Core
Heat and pressure cannot sustain life

If life exists on Neptune, it might resemble this earthly sea creature.

expel the air from a hole in the rear; that would push the animal forward in the direction it desires.

Aquatic Life on Triton?

The other place life might be found in the Neptunian system is on the largest moon—Triton. Outside of Earth, only a few bodies in the solar system have large amounts of water. One of these is Europa, one of the four largest moons of Jupiter. Most astronomers and NASA scientists believe that Europa has a liquid ocean beneath its icy outer shell. The moon's core is warm, so conditions might be right for some kind of **aquatic** (water-based) life.

Triton also has large amounts of water. Its surface consists of a thick shell of nitrogen and water ices. But liquid water almost surely existed in the interior in the past. Some of that water might still flow as a shallow ocean beneath the outer icepack. If so, some form of aquatic life may have developed there.

The shapes of the possible creatures in Triton's ocean might be familiar. This is because most aquatic life needs to be streamlined for

An artist's view shows Triton's frozen surface. A liquid ocean may exist below.

efficient motion in a liquid. So many dwellers in Triton's sea will likely be bullet or torpedo shaped, like earthly fish and dolphins. Other familiar features will be fins to steer with and some kind of mouths with which to feed. Because aquatic creatures live in a nearly weightless environment, they can grow very large. Therefore, some sea creatures on Triton might be as large as whales or even larger.

Such creatures will also need some kind of detection system. To survive, an animal must be able to find food and recognize both friends and enemies. A number of such detection systems

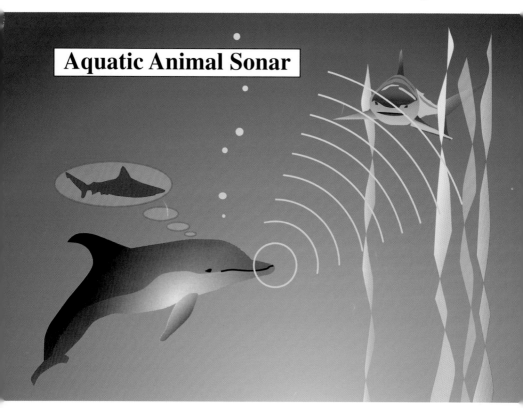

Aquatic Animal Sonar

are at work in Earth's seas. The most obvious one is sight, because most sea creatures have some kind of eyes. Dolphins and other advanced aquatic animals also use a kind of **sonar**; they send out invisible waves, which strike various objects and bounce back. In addition, some earthly sea creatures can detect magnetic fields. A number of fish use Earth's magnetism to navigate through the sea.

Tritonian sea creatures might employ some or all of these same detection systems. Or they may use less familiar ones. They might sense the positions and forms of other creatures by "seeing" the heat they give off. Or they might navigate by sending out and receiving microwaves (like those generated by microwave ovens).

The Search for Life

Such detection systems might also be used for communication, at least between members of the same species. On Earth, a few species having the ability to communicate developed some form of intelligence. (These include humans, chimps, and dolphins.)

This leads to the possibility that intelligent life might have developed on Triton. Such a concept is not impossible, of course. But it must be stressed that no proof yet exists for

On Earth, chimps are among several species that have developed a kind of intelligence.

any sort of life in Neptune's planetary system. So the idea of intelligent Neptunian life is presently a stretch of the imagination at best.

Still, someday people will likely find some kind of life somewhere in the depths of space; if it is not on Neptune, it will be somewhere else. The universe is a vast and wondrous place. And the search for life has only just begun.

Glossary

ammonia: A colorless, poisonous gas made up of the elements nitrogen and hydrogen.

aquatic: Water-based; living in the ocean.

Bode's Law: A mathematical pattern recognized by Johann Bode, a German astronomer, in the nineteenth century. He pointed out that moving outward from the sun, each known planet orbited at roughly twice the distance as the one before it.

dense: Highly compact.

dynamic: Very active or energetic; constantly in motion.

gas giant: The name given by astronomers to the planets Jupiter, Saturn, Uranus, and Neptune because they are made up mostly of gases and liquids.

gravity: A force exerted by an object that attracts other objects. The pull of Earth's gravity keeps rocks, trees, people, and houses from floating away into space. It also holds the moon in its orbit around Earth.

impact crater: A hole in the ground created by the crash of an object from space.

mass: The total amount of matter contained in an object.

methane: A gas made up of the elements carbon and hydrogen.

orbit: To move around something; or the path taken by a planet or other heavenly body around the sun, or a moon around a planet.

planet: A large solid or gaseous object orbiting the sun or another star.

planetesimals: Small objects that orbited the early sun and combined to form the planets.

retrograde motion: Movement in the opposite direction from the one considered normal.

rotate: To spin around a central axis.

spherical: Round like a ball.

solar system: The sun and all of the objects that orbit it.

sonar: Invisible waves sent out by a machine or an animal (such as a dolphin); the waves strike objects and bounce back, revealing the position and shape of the objects.

For Further Exploration

Pam Beasant, *1000 Facts About Space.* New York: Kingfisher Books, 1992. An informative collection of basic facts about the stars, planets, asteroids, and other heavenly bodies.

Larry Dane Brimner, *Neptune.* Danbury, CT: Childrens Press, 1999. A well-illustrated volume that tells most of the basic facts about the planet Neptune.

Nigel Henbest, *DK Space Encyclopedia.* London: Dorling Kindersley, 1999. This beautifully mounted and critically acclaimed book is the best general source available for grade-school readers about the wonders of space. Contains several stunning photos of Neptune.

Robin Kerrod, *The Children's Space Atlas: A Voyage of Discovery for Young Astronauts.*

Brookfield, CT: Millbrook Press, 1992. A well-written, informative explanation of the stars, planets, comets, asteroids, and other objects making up the universe.

Seymour Simon, *Neptune*. New York: William Morrow, 1991. One of the best books available for young readers about Neptune. Includes numerous photos taken by the Voyager 2 spacecraft in 1989.

Gregory L. Vogt, *Neptune*. Mankato, MN: Bridgestone Books, 2000. A very well written and nicely illustrated book for young readers by one of the leading writers about outer space.

Index